TOP HITS OF 1998

**Piano
Vocal
Guitar**

M781.64 Top 1998

Top hits of 1998 :
piano, vocal, guitar.
[1998]

EVANSTON PUBLIC LIBRARY
1703 ORRINGTON AVENUE
EVANSTON, ILLINOIS 60201

ISBN 0-634-00021-7

7777 W. BLUEMOUND RD. P.O. BOX 13819 MILWAUKEE, WI 53213
International Copyright Secured   All Rights Reserved

For all works contained herein:
Unauthorized copying, arranging, adapting, recording or public performance is an infringement of copyright.
Infringers are liable under the law.

Visit Hal Leonard Online at
www.halleonard.com

TOP HITS OF 1998

CONTENTS

Adia	4
Sarah McLachlan	
All My Life	11
K-Ci & JoJo	
The Boy Is Mine	20
Brandy & Monica	
Cruel Summer	32
Ace of Base	
Gettin' Jiggy Wit It	38
Will Smith	
I Don't Want To Wait	40
Paula Cole	
I Will Wait	48
Hootie & The Blowfish	
I'll Be	54
Edwin McCain	
Iris	60
Goo Goo Dolls	
My All	27
Mariah Carey	
My Father's Eyes	70
Eric Clapton	
My Heart Will Go On (Love Theme from 'Titanic')	76
Celine Dion	
Never Ever	82
All Saints	
Recover Your Soul	90
Elton John	
Something About the Way You Look Tonight	104
Elton John	
To Love You More	97
Celine Dion	
Torn	110
Natalie Imbruglia	
Tubthumping	118
Chumbawamba	
Uninvited	130
Alanis Morissette	
When the Lights Go Out	124
Five	

Adia

Words and Music by SARAH McLACHLAN
and PIERRE MARCHAND

Copyright © 1997 Sony/ATV Songs LLC, Tyde Music and Pierre J. Marchand
All Rights on behalf of Sony/ATV Songs LLC and Tyde Music Administered by
Sony/ATV Music Publishing, 8 Music Square West, Nashville, TN 37203
International Copyright Secured   All Rights Reserved

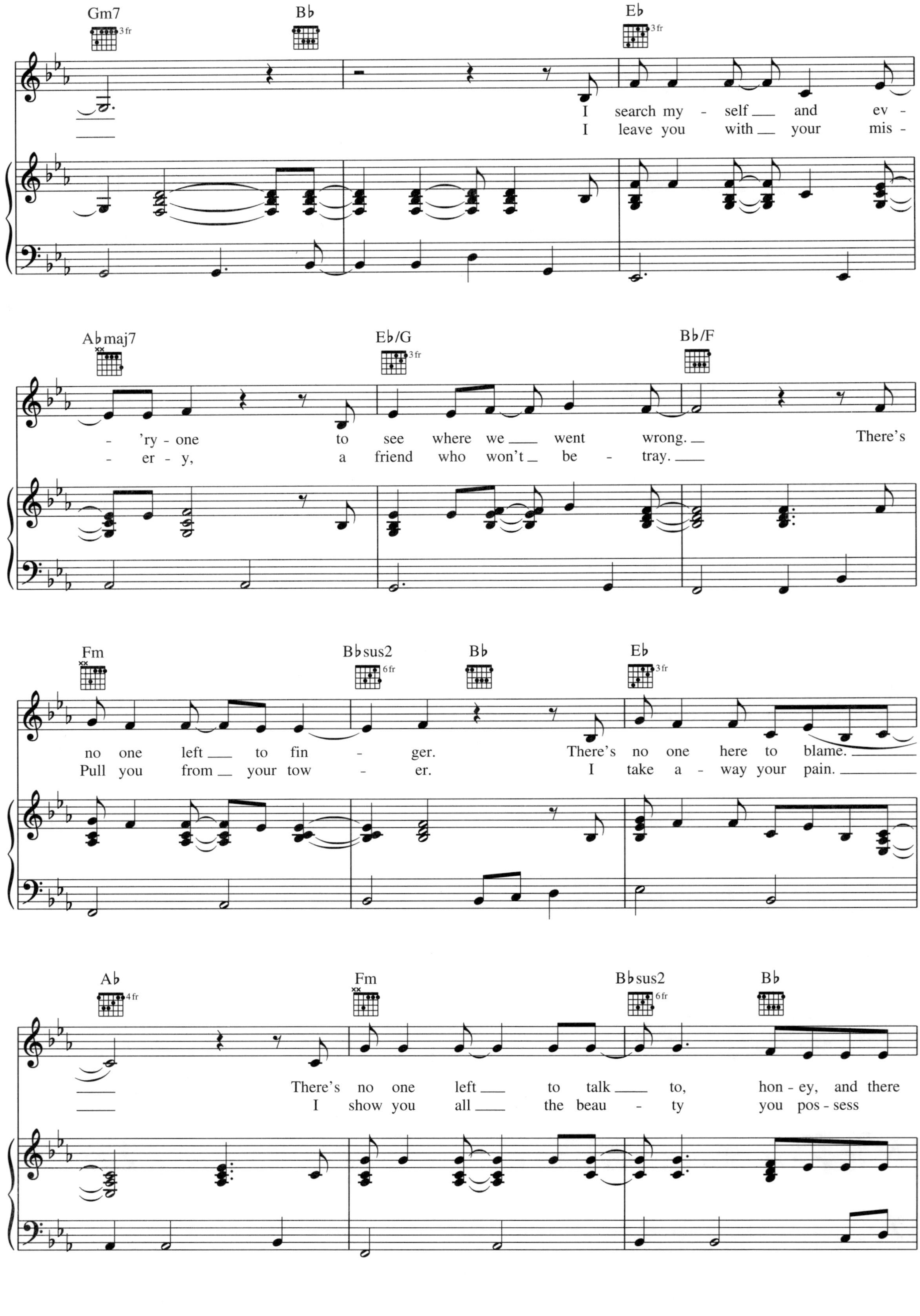
Gm7
B♭
E♭
3 fr
I search my - self and ev -
I leave you with your mis -
A♭maj7
E♭/G
B♭/F
- 'ry - one to see where we went wrong. There's
- er - y, a friend who won't be - tray.
Fm
B♭sus2
B♭
E♭
6 fr
no one left to fin - ger. There's no one here to blame.
Pull you from your tow - er. I take a - way your pain.
A♭
Fm
B♭sus2
B♭
4 fr
There's no one left to talk to, hon - ey, and there
I show you all the beau - ty you pos - sess

All My Life

Words by JOEL HAILEY
Music by JOEL HAILEY and RORY BENNETT

Original key: D♭ major. This edition has been transposed down one half-step to be more playable.

© 1997 EMI APRIL MUSIC INC., CORD KAYLA MUSIC and HEE BEE DOINIT MUSIC
All Rights for CORD KAYLA MUSIC Controlled and Administered by EMI APRIL MUSIC INC.
All Rights Reserved   International Copyright Secured   Used by Permission

The Boy Is Mine

My All

Words by MARIAH CAREY
Music by MARIAH CAREY
and WALTER AFANASIEFF

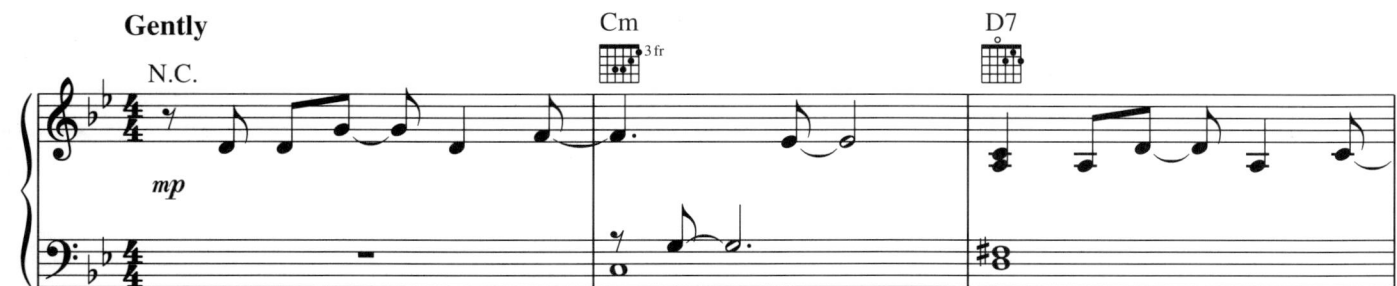

I am think-ing of _____ you _____
feel me _____
Guitar solo

A
B
Amaj7
B
Amaj7
Amaj7/B
C♯m
A
B
A
C♯m
A
Now, don't you leave me, mm.
Now, don't you leave me.
Now, don't you leave me. Come
B
A
C♯m
A
B
A
on, come on, mm.
Now, don't you leave me, mm.
Now, don't you leave me.
Amaj7
B
Amaj7
B
Now, don't you leave me. Come on, come on. It's a cruel,

C♯m A B A C♯m A
cruel summer,
(1.,2.) leav-ing me here
(3.) Vocal ad lib.
B A C♯m A B A
on my own. It's a cruel, cruel summer.
Now, you're gone.
1,2 C♯m A B A
You're not the only one. It's a cruel.
3 C♯m A B A C♯m
It's a cruel summer.

Gettin' Jiggy Wit It

Words and Music by NILE RODGERS,
BERNARD EDWARDS, WILL SMITH,
SAMUEL J. BARNES and J. ROBINSON

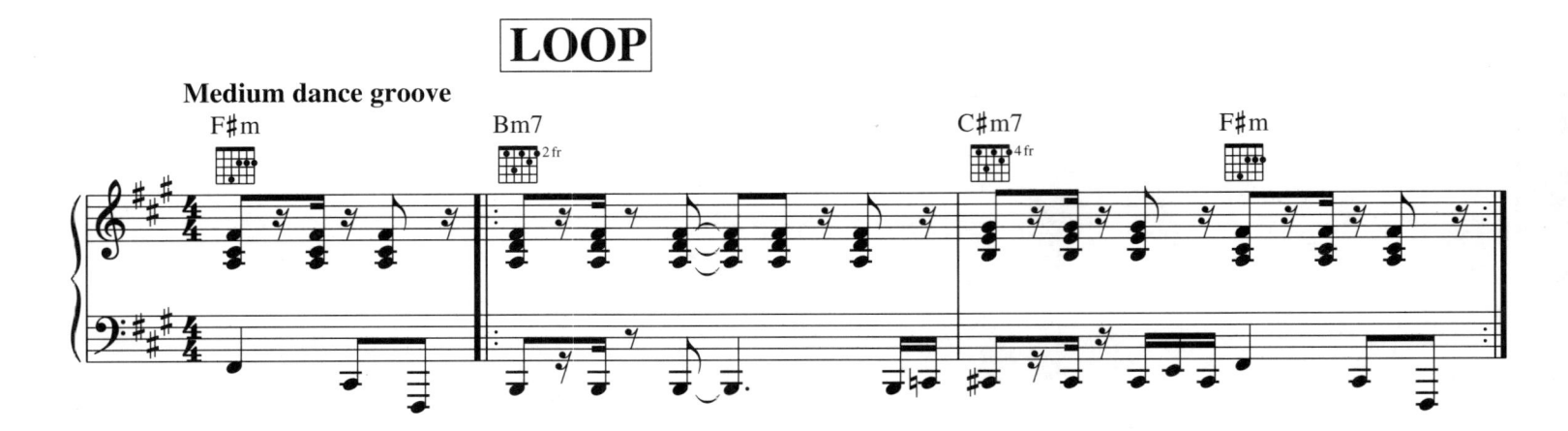

LOOP

Medium dance groove

F#m　　　Bm7　　　C#m7　　　F#m

LYRICS

Intro
(Loop)
Bring it.
Whoo!
Unh, unh, unh, unh
Hoo cah cah.
Hah hah, hah hah.
Bicka bicka bow bow bow,
Bicka bow bow bump bump.
What, what, what, what?
Hah hah hah hah.

Rap 1:
(Loop)
On your mark, ready, set, let's go.
Dance floor pro, I know you know
I go psycho when my new joint hit.
Just can't sit,
Gotta get jiggy wit it,
Ooh, that's it.
Now, honey, honey, come ride,
DKNY all up in my eye.
You gotta Prada bag with alotta stuff in it,
Give it to your friend, let's spin.
Everybody lookin' at me,
Glancin' the kid,
Wishin' they was dancin' a jig
Here with this handsome kid.
Ciga-cigar right from Cuba-Cuba,
I just bite it.
It's for the look, I don't light it.
Illway the an-may on the ance-day oor-flay,
Givin' up jiggy, make it feel like foreplay.
Yo, my car-dee-o is Infinit-
Ha, ha.
Big Willie Style's all in it,
Gettin' jiggy wit it.

Copyright © 1997 Sony/ATV Songs LLC, Warner-Tamerlane Publishing Corp., Bernard's Other Music,
Treyball Music, Slam U Well Music and Jelly's Jams, L.L.C.
All Rights on behalf of Sony/ATV Songs LLC Administered by Sony/ATV Music Publishing, 8 Music Square West, Nashville, TN 37203
International Copyright Secured   All Rights Reserved
(contains a sample of "He's The Greatest Dancer" written by Nile Rodgers and Bernard Edwards.
Copyright © 1978 Sony/ATV Songs LLC, Warner-Tamerlane Publishing Corp. and Bernard's Other Music)

Refrain: Na na na na na na na, nana
(Loop) Na na na na nana.
Gettin' jiggy wit it.
(Repeat 3x)

Rap 2: What? You wanna ball with the kid?
(Loop) Watch your step, you might fall
Trying to do what I did.
Mama-unh, mama-unh, mama come closer
In the middle of the club with the rub-a-dub, uhn.
No love for the haters, the haters,
Mad cause I got floor seats at the Lakers.
See me on the fifty yard line with the Raiders.
Met Ali, he told me I'm the greatest.
I got the fever for the flavor of a crowd pleaser.
DJ, play another
From the prince of this.
Your highness,
Only mad chicks ride in my whips.
South to the west to the east to the north,
Bought my hits and watch 'em go off, a-go off.
Ah yes, yes y'all, ya don't stop.
In the winter or the (summertime),
I makes it hot
Gettin' jiggy wit 'em.

Refrain

Rap 3: Eight-fifty I.S.; if you need a lift,
(Loop) Who's the kid in the drop?
Who else, Will Smith,
Livin' that life some consider a myth.
Rock from South Street to One Two Fifth.
Women used to tease me,
Give it to me now nice and easy
Since I moved up like George and Wheezy.
Cream to the maximum, I be askin' 'em,
"Would you like to bounce with the brother that's platinum?"
Never see Will attackin' 'em,
Rather play ball with Shaq and um,
Flatten 'em,
Psyche.
Kiddin',
You thought I took a spill
But I didn't.
Trust the lady of my life, she hittin'.
Hit her with a drop top with the ribbon,
Crib for my mom on the outskirts of Philly.
You, trying to flex on me?
Don't be silly,
Gettin' jiggy wit it.

Refrain

I Don't Want To Wait

Words and Music by
PAULA COLE

Strongly

So o-pen up your morn-ing light and say a lit-tle prayer for I. You know that if we are to stay a-live, then see the peace in ev-'ry eye. Du du du du du,

Copyright © 1996 by Ensign Music Corporation and Hingface Music
International Copyright Secured   All Rights Reserved

du du du __ du du, du du du __ du du du. __

She had two __ ba - bies,
He showed up __ all wet

one was six _ months, one _ was three, in the war _ of for - ty - four. __
on the rain - y front _ step wear - ing shrap - nel in his skin. __

Ev - 'ry tel - e - phone ring, ev - 'ry heart - beat sting - ing when she
And the war __ he saw lives _ in - side __ him still. __ It's so

Em7
D
Cmaj9
thought it was God call - ing her. Oh, would
hard to be gen - tle and warm. The years
Em
D6
C(add9)
her son grow to know his fa - ther?
pass by, and now he has grand - daugh - ters.
G(add2)
D(add4)/F#
Em11
7 fr
Dsus
I don't want to wait for our lives to be o - ver. I want
C6
G(add9)/B
Dsus/A
Dsus
to know right now, what will it be?

43

Am9♭13
the room. You're wear-ing your an-guish a - gain. Be-lieve
B♭(add2)
Fsus
C(add9)
me, I know the feel - ing; it sucks you in-to the jaws of an - ger.
G7(add4)
Oh, so breathe a lit-tle more deep-ly, my love. All we
Am9♭13
B♭(add2)
have is this ver-y mo - ment, and I don't want to do what his fa-ther and his fa-ther and

his fa-ther did. I want to be here now. So o-pen up your morn-ing light and say a lit-tle prayer for I. You know that if we are to stay a-live, then see the peace in ev-'ry eye. I don't want to wait for our lives to be o-ver. I want

C6 G(add9)/B Dsus/A Dsus G(add2) D(add4)/F#
to know right now, what will it be?
I don't want to wait for our lives
Em11 Dsus C6 G(add9)/B
7 fr
to be o - ver. Will it be yes, or will it be...
1 Dsus/A Dsus
2 Dsus/A G(add2)
sor - ry?
Du du du du du,
C6/9
du du du du du,
du du du du du du.
1

Reprise theme of "Me"

Repeat and Fade

I Will Wait

Words and Music by DARIUS RUCKER, DEAN FELBER, MARK BRYAN and JIM SONEFELD

Moderately

A-board his ship _ he stops _ to stare. _ Needs to _ smell her, touch _ her hair. Says, "I can't be with-out her."

© 1998 EMI APRIL MUSIC INC. and MONICA'S RELUCTANCE TO LOB
All Rights Controlled and Administered by EMI APRIL MUSIC INC.
All Rights Reserved   International Copyright Secured   Used by Permission

To - night he's gon - na be with - out her. "It's late now,"
left be - hind so
she says. Makes her mind up, goes to bed.
they could stay. God, to feel him, this she prays.
An - oth - er night a - lone with - out him, an - oth - er night a -
It'd make her feel so much bet - ter. I wan - na feel
lone in Charles - ton.
so much bet - ter.
When I wake to find the sol - ace of

Lyrics:

all {that / that all} we've be-come, ___ I can't wait to make the prom-is-es that I've been lear-y of. Take ___ me down, ___ let ___ me see. {I'll ___ be there, / I'll ___ be there, / I'll,___} I'll be ___ there wait-ing for you ___ in the morn-in' when times have changed. ___

I'll be there through the lies and all; I'll be stand-in' like your soldiers. And you hold your secrets through the days when I need to be alone. I will wait for you through the rise and fall.

through the rise and fall. I'll be there

wait-ing for you ___ in the morn-in' when

times have changed. (I will wait.) I will wait for you

through the rise and ___ fall. ___

I'll Be

Words and Music by
EDWIN C. McCAIN

Gently

The strands in your eyes __ that col-or them __ won-der-ful __ stop me __ and steal my __ breath.
rain falls __ an-gry on the tin roof as __ we lie __ a-wake in my bed.

And em-'ralds from moun-tains thrust towards the sky, __
And you're my sur-viv-al, you're my liv-ing proof.

Original key: B Major. This edition has been transposed up one half-step to be more playable.

© 1997 EMI APRIL MUSIC INC. and HARRINGTON PUBLISHING
All Rights Controlled and Administered by EMI APRIL MUSIC INC.
All Rights Reserved   International Copyright Secured   Used by Permission

never revealing their depth.
my love is alive and not dead.

And tell me that we belong together. Dress it up with the trappings of love. I'll be captivated, I'll hang from your lips in-stead of the gal-lows of heart-ache that hang from a-bove.

I'll be your cry-in' shoul-der, I'll be love su-i-cide. And I'll be better when I'm older, _____ I'll _____ be _____ the greatest fan of your ___ life. _____

D.S. al Coda

And

CODA

_____ And I've ___ dropped out, I've burned up. I

fought my way back from the dead. I've

tuned in, turned on, re - mem - bered the thing that you said.

I'll be your cry - in' shoul - der,

59

Iris
from the Motion Picture CITY OF ANGELS

Words and Music by
JOHN RZEZNIK

With a steady pulse

And I'd give up for-ev-er to touch you 'cause I know that you feel me some-how.
I could taste is this mo-ment, and all I can breath is your life.
fight the tears that ain't com-ing, or the mo-ment of truth in your lies.

You're the clos-est to heav-en that I'll
And soon-er or lat-er it's o-
When ev-'ry-thing feels like the mov-

© 1998 EMI VIRGIN SONGS, INC. and SCRAP METAL MUSIC
All Rights Controlled and Administered by EMI VIRGIN SONGS, INC.
All Rights Reserved   International Copyright Secured   Used by Permission

G5
3fr
Bm
ev - er be and I don't wan - na go
- ver. I just don't wan - na miss
- ies, yeah, you bleed just to know
Asus
1
G5
3fr
2,3
G5
3fr
home right now. And all
you to - night.
you're a - live.
Bm
A(add4)
G(add2)
And I don't want the world to see me
Bm
D/A
G
'cause I don't think that they'd un - der - stand.

Lyrics:

When ev-'ry-thing's made to be bro-ken I just want you to know who I am.

Bm
Bm9
Gmaj7
D.S. al Coda
(Take 2nd ending)
And you can't
CODA
N.C.
1
G
Gmaj7
2
Gmaj7
G

Bm
Bm7
2 fr
Bm
G
Gmaj7
Bm
Bm9
Bm
G
Gmaj7
Bm(add4)
Bm11
Bm(add4)
G
Gmaj7

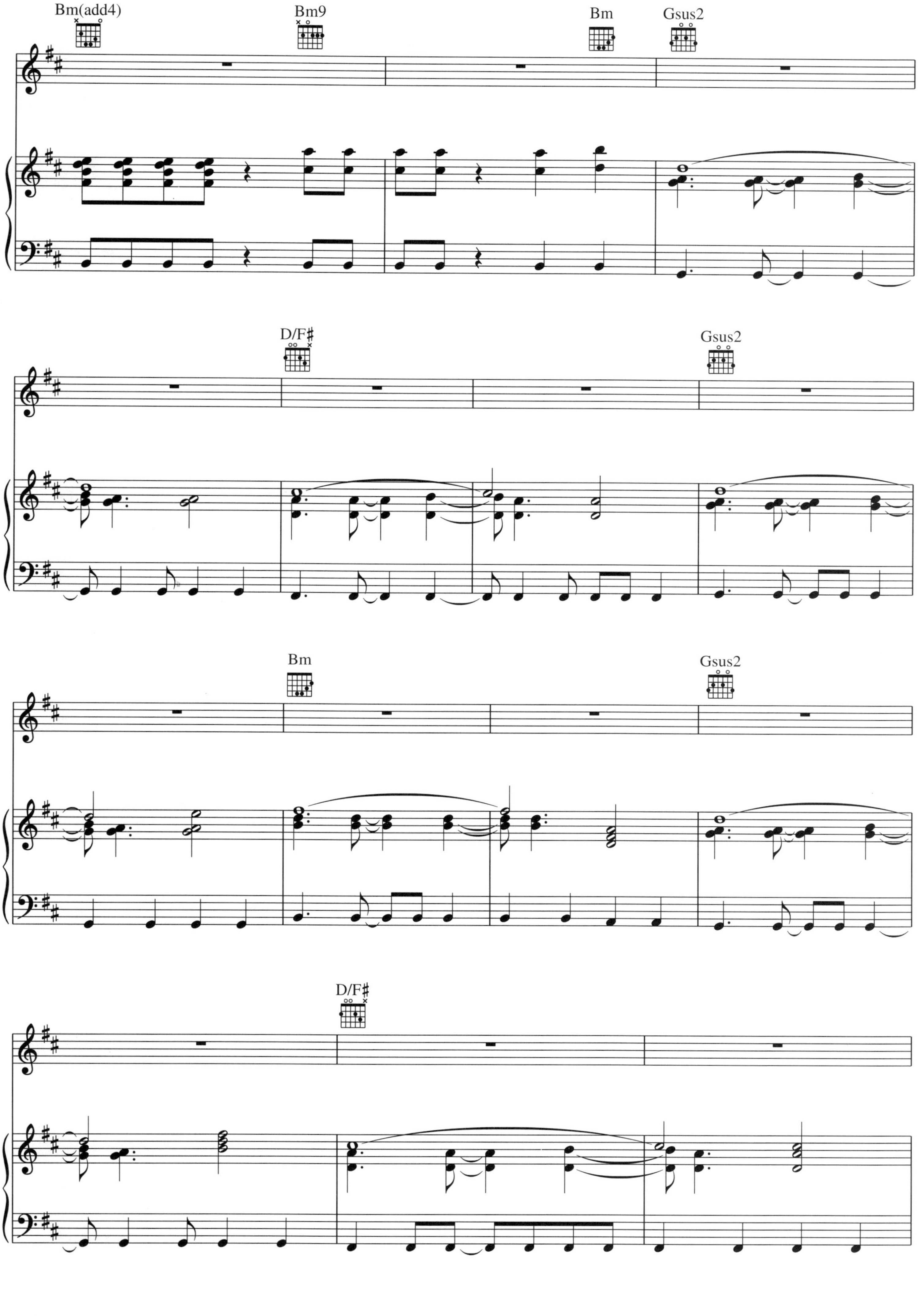
Bm(add4)
Bm9
Bm
Gsus2
D/F♯
Gsus2
Bm
Gsus2
D/F♯

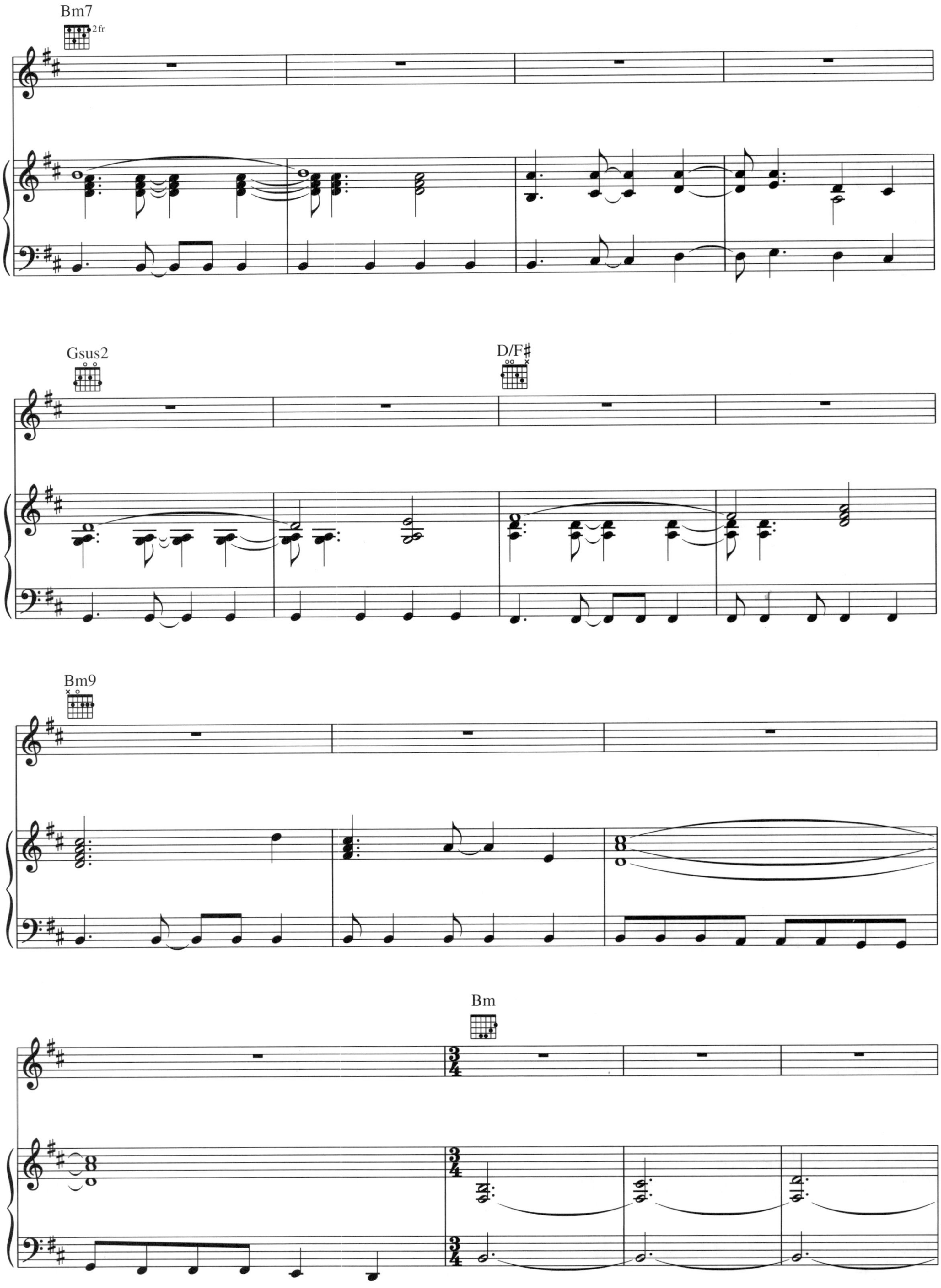
Bm7
2 fr
Gsus2
D/F♯
Bm9
Bm

And I ____ don't want the world ____ to see ____ me

Bm
D/A
G
'cause I don't think that they'd un - der - stand.
Bm
A(add4)
G
When ev - 'ry - thing's made to be bro - ken
Bm
A(add4)
I just want you to know who I
1
G
am.
And I

2
G
Bm
am.
I just want you to know
Aadd4
1,2
G
who I am.
I just want
3
Bm7
2fr
A(add4)/C♯
D5
5fr
am.
Vocal 1st time only
Bm
Asus
G5
3fr
Repeat and Fade
Optional Ending

My Father's Eyes

Words and Music by
ERIC CLAPTON

Sailing down be-
Then the light be-
Then the jag - ged

hind the sun, waiting for ___ my prince ___ to come. ___
gins to shine and I hear those an - cient lul - la - bies. ___
edge ap - pears through the dis - tant clouds _ of tears. ___

Pray - ing ___ for ___ the heal - ing rain to re - store ___ my
And as ___ I watch this seed - ling grow, feel my heart start to
And I'm like a bridge that ___ was washed a - way. My foun - da - tions were

A/E E C#m Amaj7 F#m7 B
soul a - gain. Just a toe rag on the run.
o - ver - flow. Where do I find the words to say?
made of clay. And as my soul slides down to die,
E A F#m7 B G#m7 C#m Amaj7
How did I get here? What have I done? When will all my
How do I teach him? What do we play? Bit by bit
how could I lose him? What did I try? Bit by bit
F#m7 B E A F#m7 B G#m
hopes a - rise? How will I know him when I look in
I'd re - al - ize that's when I need them that's when I need
I'd re - al - ize that he was here with me. I looked in - to
my fath - er's eyes,
C#m Amaj7 F#m7 B E A
my fath - er's eyes.
(Look in - to my fath - er's eyes.)

When I look in
That's when I need my father's eyes,
I looked into (Look in - to my father's eyes.)
my father's eyes.

C♯m
4fr
Amaj7
F♯m7
B
E
A
F♯m7
B
G♯m7
4fr
C♯m7
4fr
Amaj7
D.S. al Coda
F♯m7
B
E
A
F♯m
A
E
CODA
E
A
F♯m7
B
C♯m
4fr
Amaj7
My fath-er's eyes.
(Looked in - to my fath -

75

My Heart Will Go On
(Love Theme from 'Titanic')
from the Paramount and Twentieth Century Fox Motion Picture TITANIC

Music by JAMES HORNER
Lyric by WILL JENNINGS

Moderately

Ev-'ry night in my dreams I see you, I feel you, that is how I know you go on.

Copyright © 1997 by Famous Music Corporation, Ensign Music Corporation, TCF Music Publishing, Inc.,
Fox Film Music Corporation and Blue Sky Rider Songs
All Rights for Blue Sky Rider Songs Administered by Irving Music, Inc.
International Copyright Secured   All Rights Reserved

E
B
Asus2
Far a-cross the dis-tance and spac-es be-
E/B
B
E
B
A
tween us you have come to show you go on.
C♯m
4 fr
B(add4)
A
Near, far, wher-ev-er you are,
B
C♯m
4 fr
B(add9)
7 fr
A
I be-lieve that the heart does go on.

Once more you o-pen the door and you're here in my heart, and my heart will go on and on.

Love can touch us one time and last for a

life - time, and nev-er let go till we're gone.

Love was when I loved you; one true time I hold to. In my life we'll al-ways go on.

D.S. al Coda

CODA

on.

You're here, there's nothing I fear ___ and I know ___ that my heart will go on. ___ We'll stay for-ev - er this way. You are safe in my heart, and my heart will go on and on.

Mm.

Never Ever

Words and Music by SHAZNAY LEWIS,
SEAN MATHER and ROBERT JAZAYERI

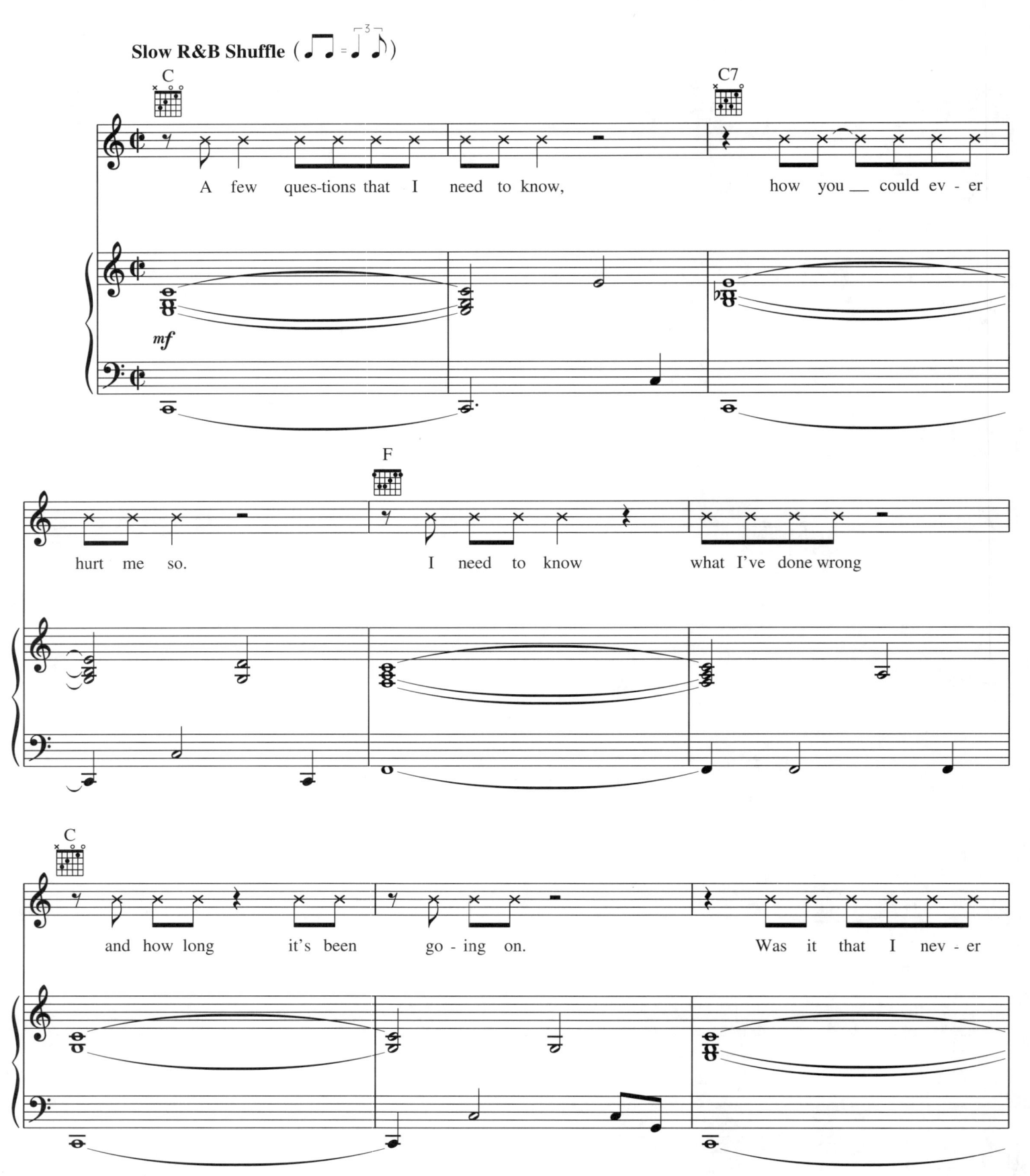

Slow R&B Shuffle

A few questions that I need to know, how you could ever hurt me so. I need to know what I've done wrong and how long it's been going on. Was it that I never

Original key: D♭ major. This edition has been transposed down one half-step to be more playable.

© Copyright 1998 by MCA MUSIC LTD. and RICKIDY RAW MUSIC
All Rights for MCA MUSIC LTD. in the Western Hemisphere Controlled and Administered by MCA MUSIC PUBLISHING, A Division of UNIVERSAL STUDIOS, INC.
All Rights for RICKIDY RAW MUSIC in the World Controlled by MUSIK-EDITION DISCOTON GMBH
All Rights for MUSIK-EDITION DISCOTON GMBH in the United States Administered by BMG SONGS, INC.
International Copyright Secured   All Rights Reserved
MCA Music Publishing

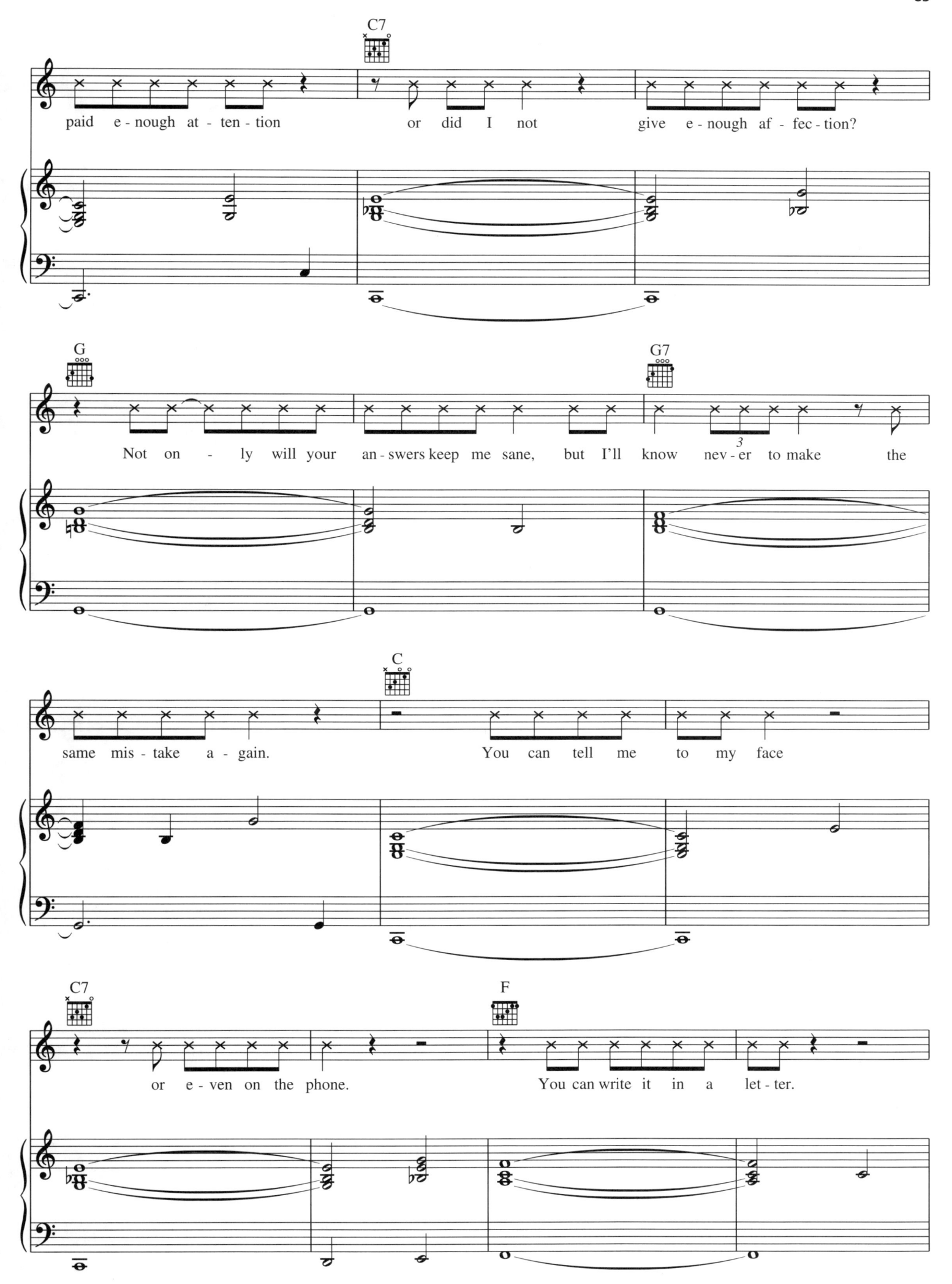

paid enough attention or did I not give enough affection?

Not only will your answers keep me sane, but I'll know never to make the same mistake again. You can tell me to my face or even on the phone. You can write it in a letter.

Either way, I have to know. Did I never treat you right? Did I always start the fight? Either way, I'm going outta my mind. All the answers to my questions, I have to find. My head's spinning. I'll keep searching

[Sheet music, page 85]

C7   **F**

Boy, I'm in ___ a daze. ___ I feel i - so - lat -
deep with - in ___ my soul ___ for all the an -

B♭/F   **C**

- ed.   Don't wan - na com - mu - ni - cate. ___
- swers.   Don't wan - na hurt ___ no more. ___

I'll take a show - er. I will ___ scour. ___ I will roam ___
I need peace, got - ta feel at ease. Need to be ___

G

to find piece of mind, the hap - py mind
free from ___ pain, not go in - sane.

I once owned, yeah. Flexing vocabulary
My heart aches, yeah. Sometimes vocabulary

runs right through me.
runs through my head.
The alphabet runs right from A to Z. / Zed.

Conversations, hesitations in my mind. You got my conscience asking

questions that I can't find. I'm not crazy. I'm

sure I ain't done noth-ing wrong. — but — I'm just wait-
ing. wrong. — And now, I'm just
wait-ing 'cause I heard that this feel-ing won't last — that long. —

Nev-er, ev-er have I ev-er felt so low. When you gon-na take me out of this black hole? Nev-er, ev-er have I ev-er felt so sad.

88

The way I'm feeling, yeah, you got me feeling really bad. Never, ever have I had to find I've had to dig away to find my own piece of mind. I've never, ever had my conscience to fight. The way I'm feeling, yeah, it

1. just don't feel right.
2. just don't feel right.

D.S. al Coda

CODA

just don't feel right. You could tell

Cm6/9

me to my face. You could tell me on the phone. Ooh, you could write it in a letter, babe, 'cause I really need to know. You could write it in a letter, babe.

Repeat and Fade

Optional Ending

Recover Your Soul

Words and Music by ELTON JOHN
and BERNIE TAUPIN

Moderately slow

Ba-by, you're miss-ing some-thing in the air.

I got a name, but it don't mat-

Copyright © 1996 by William A. Bong Limited (PRS) and Wretched Music (ASCAP)
All Rights for William A. Bong Limited Administered by Warner-Tamerlane Publishing Corp. (BMI)
All Rights for Wretched Music Administered by WB Music Corp. (ASCAP)
International Copyright Secured   All Rights Reserved

-ter. What's goin' on? It's cold in here. You have a life but it's torn and tattered.

Maybe you're losin' pieces of your heart.
Lazy old sunset, sinkin' like a tear,

Em7
C
You have a world _ but
a - lone at night _
G/B
D
it stopped turn - in'.
in a los - in' bat - tle.
C
You lose the day
That per - fect world
B7
Em
and gain the dark.
can nev - er clear.

Love was a fire but
You have to fight for the things that

it stopped burnin.'
mat - ter.

Spare your heart, save your soul, don't drag your love across the coals. Find your fate and your for-

G D
- tune can be told. Re - lease,
Am7 B7 Em
(Re-lease,) re - lax, (re - lax.) let go.
C D G7
To Coda
And hey, now let's re -
C/G D G D/G Em
cov - er your soul.

C
G/B
Am7
1
2
D.S. al Coda
Spare your heart,
CODA
C/G
D
G7
C/G
cov - er, and hey, now let's re - cov - er, hey,
D
G7
C/G
D
G
now let's re - cov - er your soul.

hey, now __ let's re - cov - er your _____ soul.

To Love You More

Words and Music by JUNIOR MILES
and DAVID FOSTER

D E A Am
Touch me once a - gain and re -
G Gm 3 fr Dm A
mem - ber when there was no one that you want - ed
Esus E A
more. Don't go, you know you'll
See me as if you
E F♯m
break my heart. She won't
nev - er know. Hold me

love you _____ like I will. _____ I'm the
so you _____ can't let go. _____ Just be-

one who'll stay _____ when she walks a-way, _____
lieve in me. _____ I will make you see _____

_____ and you know _____ I'll be stand-ing here still. _____
all the things _____ that your heart _____ needs to know. _____

I'll be wait-ing for you _____ here in-side _____ my heart. _____

C♯m
D
A/E
E
I'm the one who wants to love you more.
A
Esus
E
A
E
(1., 2.) You will
(D.S.) Can't you
see I can give you
F♯m
C♯m
D
ev - 'ry - thing you need. Let me be the one to love
A/E
E
To Coda
A
you more.
A

And some way, all the love that we had can be saved. What-ev-er it takes, we'll find a way.

D/F♯
C/E
G/D
C6
F/A
E/G♯
A
Be - lieve in me.
Am
G
Gm
3 fr
Dm
I will make you see all the things that your heart
A
E
Esus
N.C.
D.S. al Coda
needs to know. I'll be
CODA
A

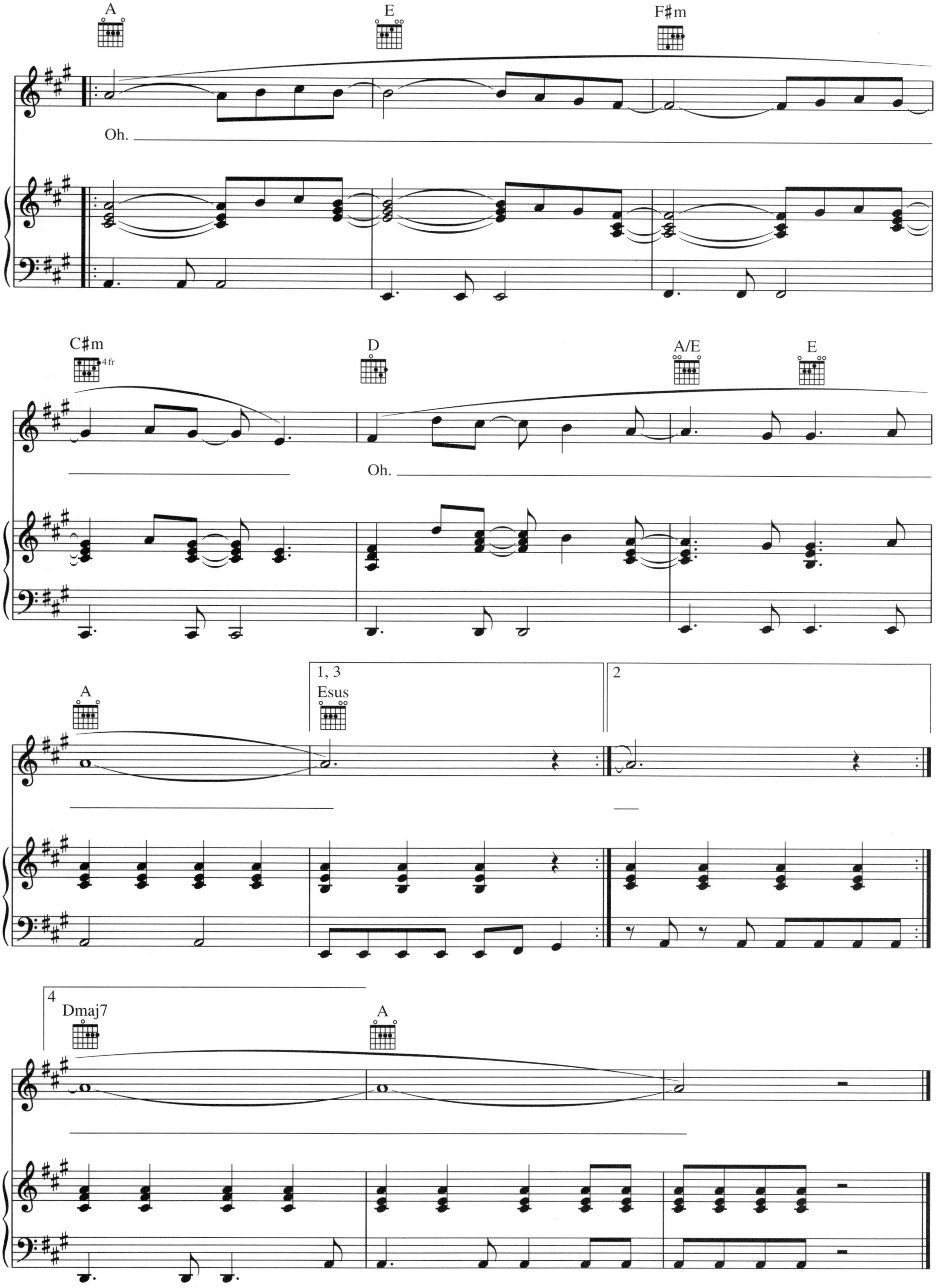
A
E
F♯m
Oh.
C♯m
4 fr
D
A/E
E
Oh.
A
1, 3
Esus
2
4
Dmaj7
A

Something About the Way You Look Tonight

Words and Music by ELTON JOHN and BERNIE TAUPIN

Slowly

There was a time I was ev'ry-thing and noth-ing all in one.

When you found me,

tell you smile, light up ev-'ry sec-ond of the day,

but in the moon-light,

how you pull the deep-est se-crets from my heart.

In all hon-es-ty,

Original Key: F-sharp major. This edition has been transposed down one half-step to be more playable.

Copyright © 1996 by William A. Bong Limited (PRS) and Wretched Music (ASCAP)
All Rights for William A. Bong Limited Administered by Warner-Tamerlane Publishing Corp. (BMI)
All Rights for Wretched Music Administered by WB Music Corp. (ASCAP)
International Copyright Secured   All Rights Reserved

Gm7
3 fr
I was feel - ing like a cloud a - cross the sun.
you just shine like a bea - con of the bay.
I'm speech - less and I don't know where to start.
C F/C C
1
F/C C
Well, I need to
2,3
F/C C
F Bb/F F
And I can't ex - plain,
A7
but there's some-thing a - bout the way you

look tonight, takes my breath away. It's that feeling I get about you deep inside. And I can't describe, but there's some-thing a-bout ___ the way ___ you look to-night, ___ takes my breath a-way. ___

The way you look ___ to-night.

N.C.
F
C
D.S. al Coda
With that
CODA
C
Bb/F
F
Bb/F
F
night,
Ab
Bb
F
the way you look to - night,
the way you
Ab
Bb
F
look to - night,
the way you look to - night,
Ab
Bb
F
4fr

the way you look to - night, _____ the way you look _____ to - night, _____ the way you look to - night, _____ the way you look to - night, _____ the way you look _____ to - night. _____

Torn

Words and Music by PHIL THORNALLEY,
ANNE PREVIN and SCOTT CUTLER

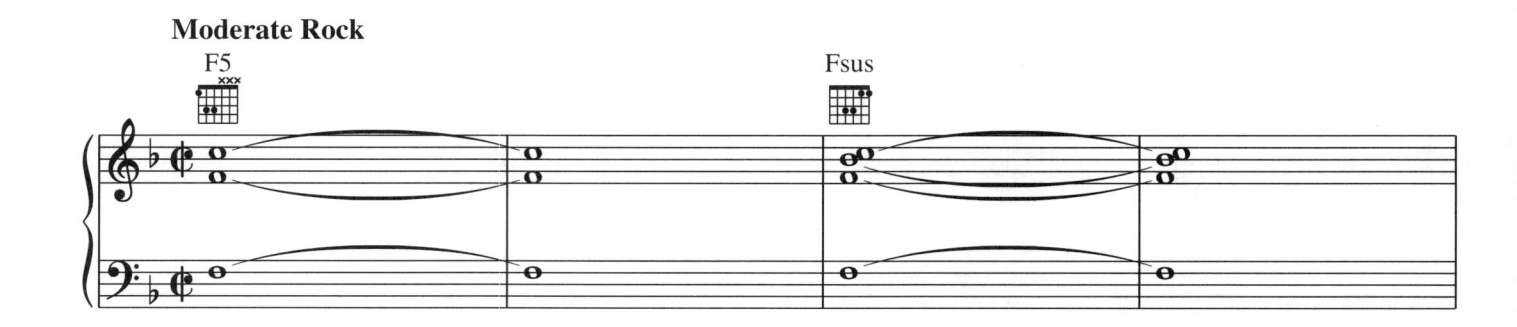

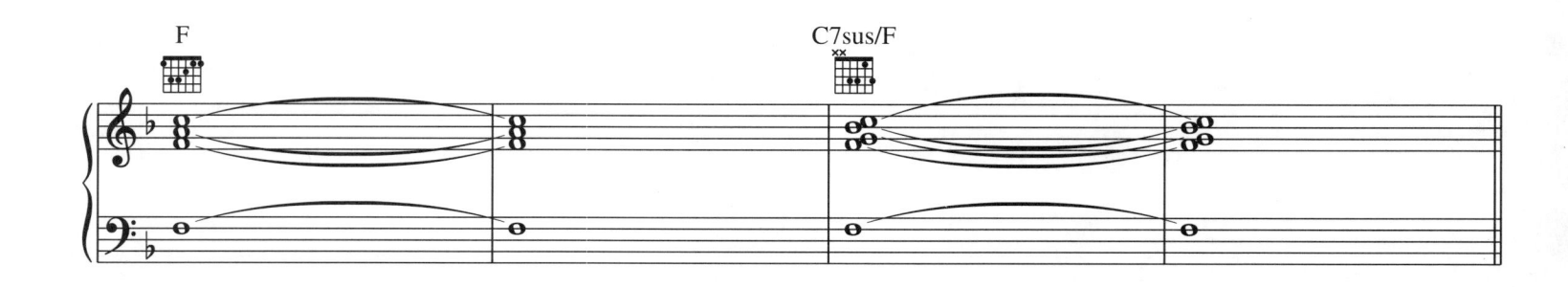

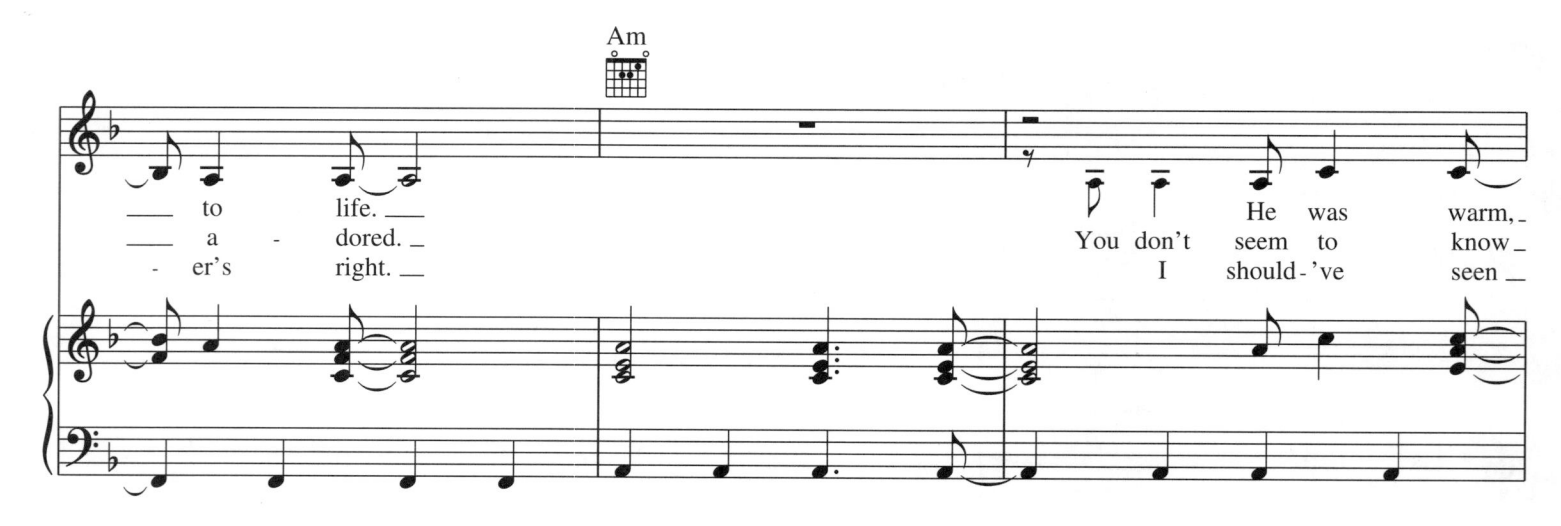

Moderate Rock

Well, you I thought I saw a man brought
So, I guess the for-tune tell-

to life.
— a - dored.
—er's right.
You don't seem to He was warm,
I should've seen know

Copyright © 1995, 1996 by BMG Music Publishing Ltd., Songs Of PolyGram International, Inc.,
Weetie-Pie Music, Colgems-EMI Music Inc. and Scott Cutler Music
All Rights for BMG Music Publishing Ltd. in the U.S. Administered by BMG Songs, Inc.
All Rights for Scott Cutler Music Controlled and Administered by Colgems-EMI Music Inc.
International Copyright Secured   All Rights Reserved

Bb7

___ he came a-round ___ like he was dig-ni-fied. ___
___ or seem to care ___ what your heart ___ is for. ___
___ just what was there ___ and not some hol-y light. ___

[1]

He showed me what it was ___ to cry.
Well, I don't know him an-
But you crawled be-neath my veins ___

[2, 3] *Dm*

-y-more.
___ and now

There's noth-ing where ___ he used to lie. ___
I don't care, ___ I have no luck. ___

C   *Am*

My con-ver-sa-tion has run dry.
I don't miss it all that much.
                                     That's
                                     There's

what's going on. _____ Nothing's fine, _____ I'm torn. _____
just so many things that I _____ can't touch, _____

I'm all out of faith, _____ this is how I feel. _____

I'm cold and I am shamed _____ lying na-

-ked on the floor. _____ Illusion never changed

C
Dm
into something real.
I'm wide awake and I
B♭
F
can see the perfect sky is torn.
You're
C
a little late.
I'm already torn.
Dm
B♭
To Coda
D.S. al Coda
(Take 2nd ending)

CODA
Dm
C
B♭(add2)
Torn.
Dm
Ooh,
F
C
ooh.
Dm
C
There's noth-ing where he used to lie.
My in - spi - ra - tion

Am
C
has run dry. That's what's go - ing on. Noth -
F
C
- ing's right, I'm torn. I'm all out of faith, this
Dm
is how I feel. I'm cold and I am shamed,
I'm a - shamed,
B♭
F
ly - ing na - ked on the floor. Il - lu -
bound and bro - ken on the floor. You're

-sion nev-er changed ___ in-to some-thing real. ___
__ a lit-tle late. ___ I'm __

I'm wide a-wake __ and I __ can see __ the per-

-fect sky is torn. ___ al-read-y torn. ___

Torn. ___

I ain't sorry for the way I feel. I know you think I'm be-ing in-sin-cere
I know you think it may be just a lie. Ain't no good in put-ting up a fight

from the way I'm treat-ing you.
'cause my heart's set on you.

I nev-er want-ed to be so un-kind. The on-ly one thing on my mind
I see the truth, it's in your eyes. I ain't fooled by your thin dis-guise.

B♭
B♭/C
is just kick - ing it with you, girl.
I can see I'm get - ting through, babe.
B♭maj7
C
Gm9
Ooh, ba - by, it's not the way I feel.
Ooh, girl, don't de - ny the way you feel.
B♭maj7
C
You know you must be-lieve me.
You know you got - ta trust me.
(You must be - lieve.)
(You got - ta trust.)
Ba - by, it's not part of the deal,
Give me a chance to prove I'm real,
C/D
D
N.C.
oh, no, no.
oh, yeah, yeah.
Ba - by, when the

lights go out ev - 'ry sin - gle word could not ex - press the love and ten - der-ness. I'll show you what it's all a - bout. Babe, I swear you will suc - cumb to me. So, ba - by, come to me when the lights go out. *(Spoken:)* Uh yeah, check it, check it out. Second verse, girl. me. Ba - by, when the

CODA

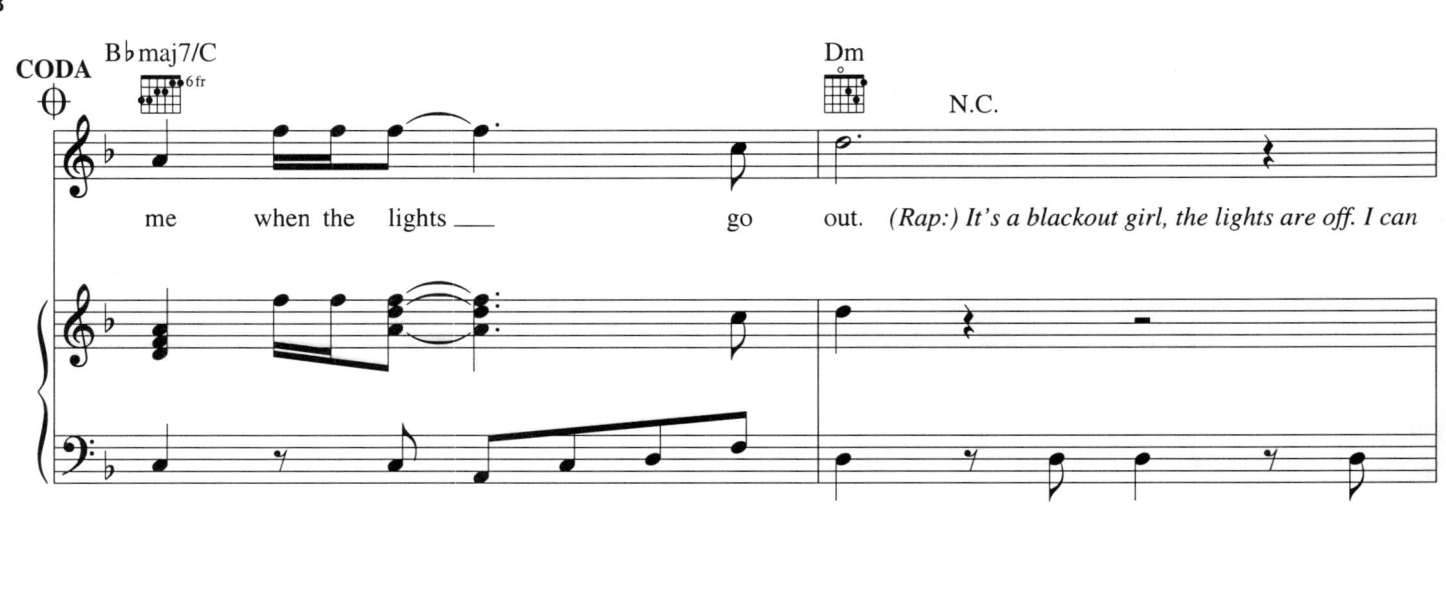

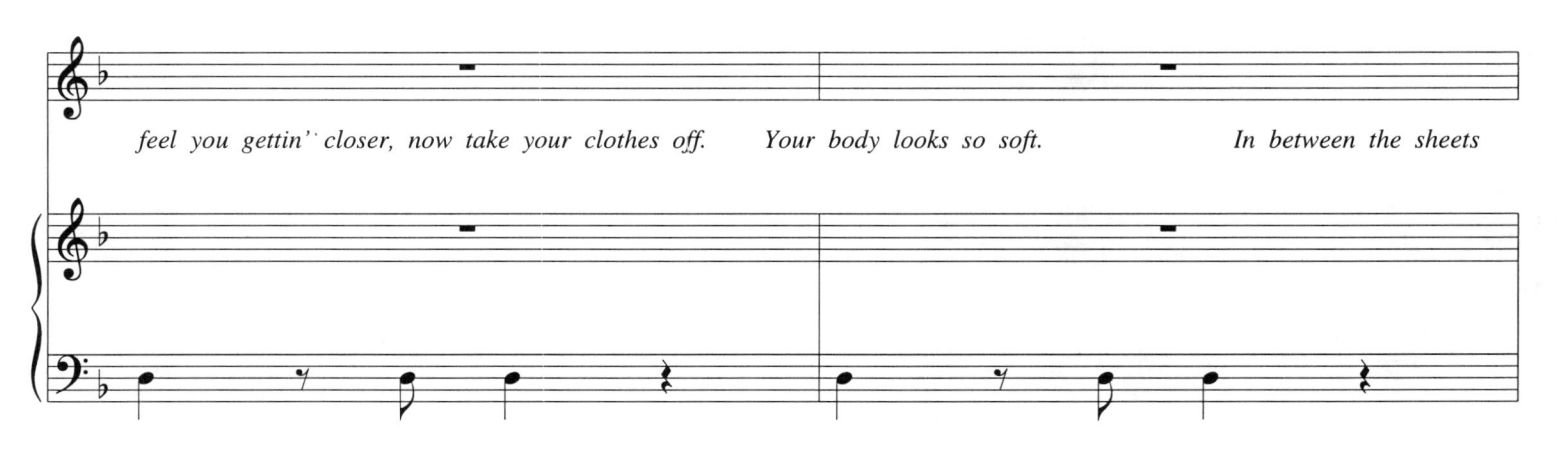

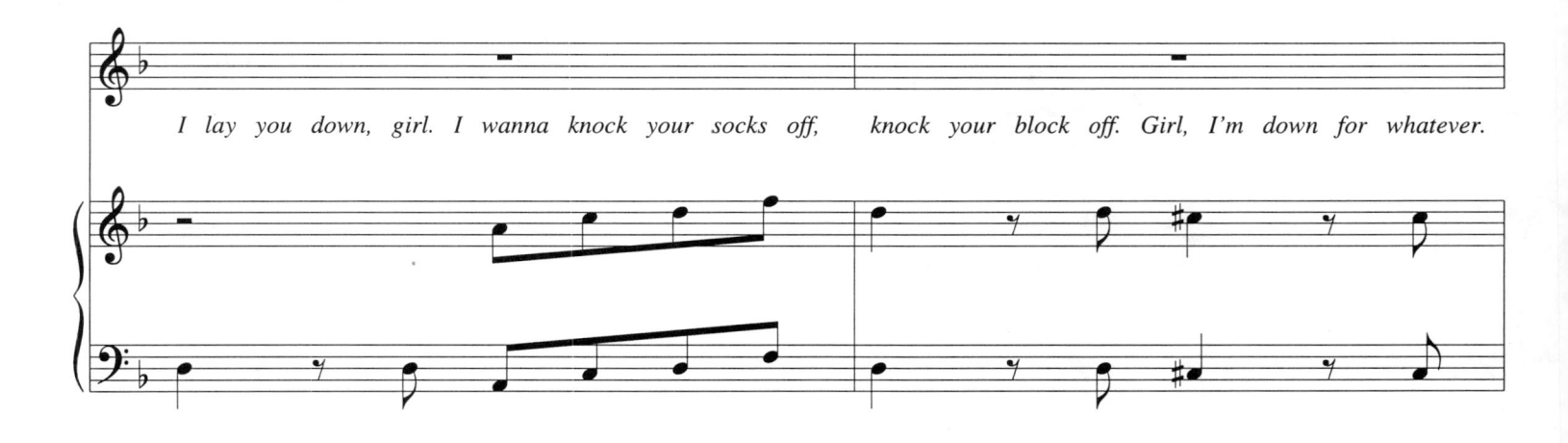

me when the lights go out. *(Rap:) It's a blackout girl, the lights are off. I can feel you gettin' closer, now take your clothes off. Your body looks so soft. In between the sheets I lay you down, girl. I wanna knock your socks off, knock your block off. Girl, I'm down for whatever. There are few things that's forever, like you in my life, girl, that's all that I need to get by.*

Time to break it down 'cause you're makin' me high.

Ba-by, when the lights go out ev-'ry sin-gle word could not ex-press the love and ten-der-ness. I'll show you what it's all a-bout. Babe, I swear you will suc-cumb to me. So, ba-by, come to me. Ba-by, when the me.

Repeat and Fade

Optional Ending

Uninvited

from the Motion Picture CITY OF ANGELS

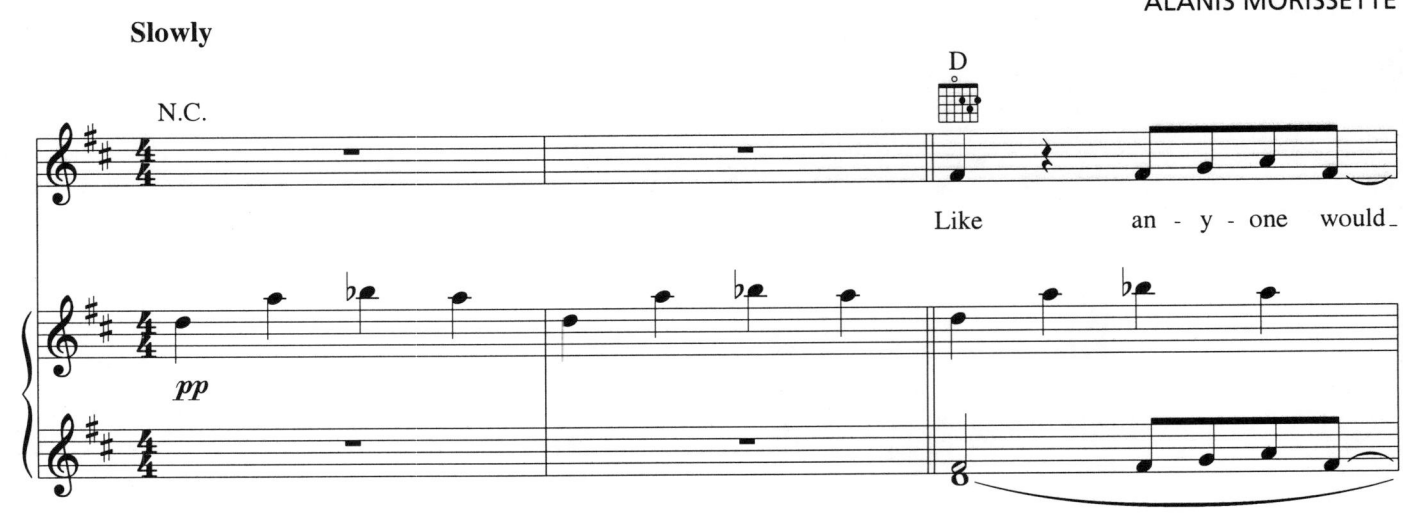

Words and Music by
ALANIS MORISSETTE

Slowly

Like anyone would be, I am flattered by your fascination with me.

Like any hot-blooded woman, I have simply

© Copyright 1998 by MUSIC CORPORATION OF AMERICA, INC. and VANHURST PLACE MUSIC
All Rights Controlled and Administered by MUSIC CORPORATION OF AMERICA, INC.
International Copyright Secured   All Rights Reserved
MCA Music Publishing

wanted an object to crave. But you, you're not allowed; you're uninvited: an unfortunate slight.

Must be strangely exciting to watch the stoic squirm.
Like any uncharted territory, I must seem greatly intriguing.

Must be somewhat heart-en-ing to watch shepherd meet shepherd.

You speak of my love like you have exper-ienced love like mine before.

But you, you're not allowed; you're uninvited: an unfortunate slight.

But this is not allowed; you're uninvited: an unfortunate slight.

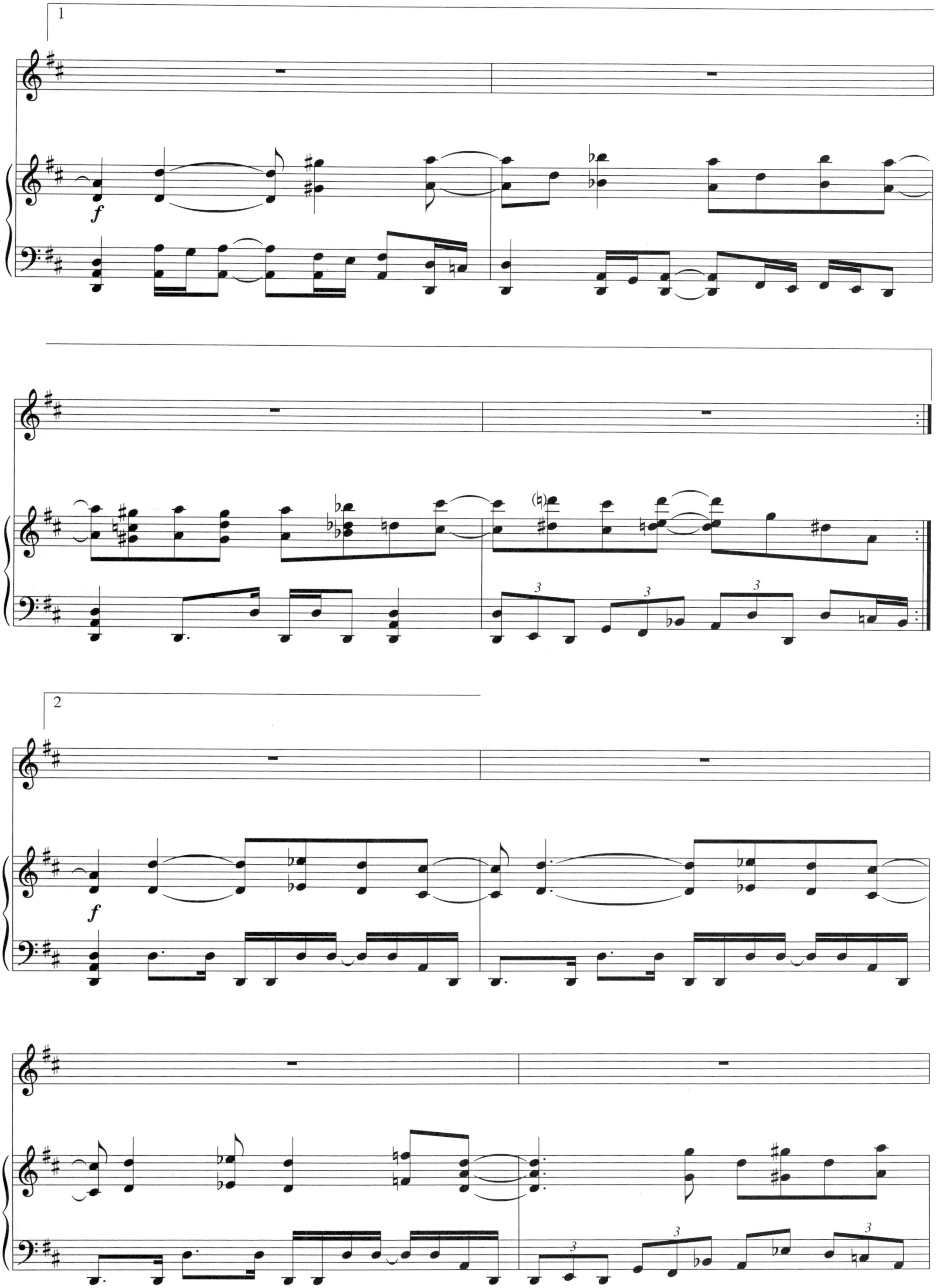
1
f
3
3
3
2
f
3
3
3

I don't think you un-wor-thy; I need a mo-ment to de-lib-er-ate.

Guitar solo ad lib.

Play 4 times